"95"

Merry Christm
Holly
Love Wendy
XOXO

# Mary Engelbreit's "Recipe for Happiness"

# Mary Engelbreit's
# "Recipe for Happiness"

Art copyright © 1992
Mary Engelbreit

Edited by Jill Wolf
Text copyright © 1992
Antioch Publishing Company
ISBN 0-89954-834-2

Printed in the U.S.A.

Note: Some measurements in parentheses
are British Imperial measure.

AN ANTIOCH GOURMET GIFT BOOK

# ❧ Mary Engelbreit's ❧ "Recipe for Happiness"

### Art by Mary Engelbreit
### Edited by Jill Wolf

Antioch Publishing Company
Yellow Springs, Ohio 45387

*A meal prepared by a person who loves you*
*will do more good than any average cooking.*
—Luther Burbank

# ❧ CONTENTS ❧

## Crudités

*Vegetables:*
*carrot and celery sticks*
*green bell pepper strips*
*cauliflower florets*
*broccoli florets*
*asparagus spears*
*radishes*
*cherry tomatoes*
*cucumber spears*
*mushrooms*

*Dip:*
*1 cup (8 fl. oz.) lowfat cottage cheese*
*1 cup (8 fl. oz.) plain lowfat yogurt or yogurt cheese*
*1 tbsp. ($^3/_4$ Br. tbsp.) chopped chives*
*1 tsp. ($^3/_4$ Br. tsp.) dill weed*
*$^1/_4$ tsp. ground black pepper*

Prepare vegetables and chill. Stir together the dip ingredients; blend well. Chill dip in refrigerator for at least 2 hours before serving with vegetables.

*I know well that happiness is in little things . . .*
—*John Ruskin*

# Mexican-Italian Pizza

1 10-inch flour tortilla
    (sold refrigerated in dairy section)
2 Roma tomatoes, sliced very thin
2 1/4-oz. can sliced black olives
2 tbsp. (1 1/2 Br. tbsp.) chopped
    green bell pepper
1 tbsp. (3/4 Br. tbsp.) minced onion
    or chopped green onion
3 ounces shredded Monterey Jack cheese
2 tsp. (1 1/2 Br. tsp.) extra virgin olive oil
1 tsp. (3/4 Br. tsp.) oregano (or basil)
ground black pepper to taste

Preheat oven to 475° F. Place tortilla on baking
sheet. Arrange tomato slices on tortilla, leaving
a margin at edge of tortilla. Add olives, pepper,
and onion. Cover with shredded cheese. Drizzle
on oil; sprinkle with oregano and pepper. Bake
about 6 minutes (until cheese melts), then broil
for about 3 minutes (until lightly browned). Cut
into quarters with a thin, sharp knife or pizza
cutter.

*Variety's the very spice of life.*
    *—William Cowper*

# Seasoned Popcorn

1/4 cup (2 fl. oz.) melted unsalted butter
1/8 tsp. garlic powder
1/2 tsp. oregano
8 cups (64 fl. oz.) freshly popped corn
1/2 cup (4 fl. oz.) grated Parmesan cheese

Stir together butter, garlic powder, and oregano.
Pour seasoned butter over popcorn in a large
bowl and toss to coat kernels. Add cheese and
toss well. Serve immediately.

*To make the world a friendly place,*
*One must show it a friendly face.*
*—James Whitcomb Riley*

## RECIPE FOR HAPPINESS

Combine 4 parts of Contentment, 2 parts of Joy & 1 part Pleasure. But these ingredients must be Grown in one's own garden. Sometimes they may be obtained of a Good Friend. When so procured, a fair return must be made else Happiness spoils & becomes trouble.

Sometimes Discontent & Ambition have been combined in a desire to obtain Happiness but Fame or Wealth have resulted and Persons who have tasted these say they are inferior substitutes.

# Gazpacho

1 clove garlic
2 cups (16 fl. oz.) peeled, chopped fresh tomatoes
1 large cucumber, pared and chopped
1/2 cup (4 fl. oz.) diced green pepper
1/2 cup (4 fl. oz.) chopped green onion
1/4 cup (2 fl. oz.) chopped black olives
2 cups (16 fl. oz.) or more tomato juice
3 tbsp. (2 1/4 Br. tbsp.) olive oil
2 tbsp. (1 1/2 Br. tbsp.) vinegar or red wine
salt and pepper to taste
dash of Tabasco

Cut garlic in half and rub over bottom and sides of a large bowl. Add tomatoes, cucumber, green pepper, onion, olives, tomato juice, olive oil, and vinegar to bowl. Stir until thoroughly mixed. Season mixture to taste with salt, pepper, and Tabasco. Chill soup in refrigerator at least 1 hour before serving.

*Soup Tip: An easy way to remove fat from soup stock is to make the stock ahead, then chill it in the refrigerator overnight. The fat congeals on the surface and is easily lifted out with a spatula.*

*There is no place more delightful than home.*
—Cicero

# Chicken-Rice Soup

3-lb. chicken
$^1/_2$ tsp. ground black
  pepper
salt to taste
celery leaves, still attached
  to tip of stalk
1 cup (8 fl. oz.) chopped
  onion
1 tbsp. ($^3/_4$ Br. tbsp.) dried
  parsley

2 tsp. (1 $^1/_2$ Br. tsp.) dill
  weed
6 large carrots, cut
  julienne-style
3 stalks celery, chopped
1 $^1/_2$ cups (12 fl. oz.)
  uncooked white rice

Wash chicken and place in kettle. Cover with cold
water; add pepper, salt, and celery leaves. Bring
water to boil. Cover kettle; lower heat and simmer
chicken for 1 $^1/_2$ hours. Remove celery leaves and
chicken. Cool chicken; bone and cut in pieces. Skim
fat from soup stock and strain. Add cut-up chicken,
onion, and herbs to stock. Heat to boiling, then add
carrots and celery. Cover; cook on medium heat for
about 20 minutes. Add rice and continue cooking
until rice is tender (about 15-20 minutes). Serve.

*A loving heart is the truest wisdom.*
*—Charles Dickens*

# Mushroom Soup

| | |
|---|---|
| 1 lb. fresh mushrooms | 1 clove minced garlic |
| 6 tbsp. (4 ½ Br. tbsp.) unsalted butter | 2 tsp. (1 ½ Br. tsp.) dried parsley |
| 2 ½ cups (20 fl. oz.) chicken broth | 1 cup (8 fl. oz.) chopped onion |
| 3 ¾ cups (30 fl. oz.) water | 2 cups (16 fl. oz.) chopped celery |
| ¼ tsp. salt | |
| ¼ tsp. ground black pepper | 2 cups (16 fl. oz.) chopped carrots |
| celery leaves, still attached to tip of stalk | 3 tbsp. (2 ¼ Br. tbsp.) cooking sherry (optional) |

Clean half of mushrooms; chop up. In a large saucepan, sauté chopped mushrooms in 4 tbsp. (3 Br. tbsp.) of butter for 5 minutes. Add broth, water, salt, pepper, and celery leaves. Bring mixture to boil; add garlic, parsley, onion, celery, and carrots. Cover; reduce heat. Simmer for 1 hour. Remove celery leaves. Puree soup in small batches in blender, taking care with hot soup. Return to saucepan. Clean remaining mushrooms; cut into lengthwise slices. Sauté sliced mushrooms in remaining butter in a small saucepan for 5 minutes. Add them to the soup (and stir in sherry, if desired). Heat to serving temperature.

*If the world seems cold to you,*
*Kindle fires to warm it!*
*—Lucy Larcom*

LIFE IS JUST A CHAIR OF BOWLIES

## Salad Niçoise

Dressing:

4 tbsp. (3 Br. tbsp.) extra
   virgin olive oil
1 tbsp. (³/₄ Br. tbsp.) red
   wine vinegar or cider
   vinegar
1 clove minced garlic

1 tsp. (³/₄ Br. tsp.) Dijon
   mustard
¹/₂ tsp. dried tarragon
¹/₂ tsp. dried basil
¹/₄ tsp. dried thyme
salt and pepper to taste

Salad Ingredients:

4 large romaine lettuce
   leaves
1 lb. fresh green beans
   (cooked, drained, and
   cooled)
4 small red-skinned
   potatoes (cooked,
   drained, cooled, and
   sliced)
1 green bell pepper, sliced
1 red bell pepper, sliced

12 cherry tomatoes,
   halved
1 2-oz. can anchovy filets
   or 1 6-oz. can tuna
6 black olives
1 small red onion, sliced
2 tbsp. (1 ¹/₂ Br. tbsp.) fresh
   parsley
3 hard-cooked eggs,
   quartered

*Write it on your heart that every day is the
best day in the year.*
                              —Ralph Waldo Emerson

18

Whisk together the dressing ingredients in a bowl until well blended; chill. Arrange lettuce, beans, potatoes, peppers, and tomatoes in a salad bowl. Top with fish, olives, onion, parsley, and eggs. Whisk dressing again; drizzle over salad. Toss before serving. Serve with French bread.

# Tangy Potato Salad

2 lbs. red-skinned potatoes
1 tbsp. ($^3/_4$ Br. tbsp.) olive oil
1 tbsp. ($^3/_4$ Br. tbsp.) red wine vinegar or cider vinegar
$^1/_2$ cup (4 fl. oz ) mayonnaise
$^1/_2$ cup (4 fl. oz.) plain loufat yogurt
1 tbsp. ($^3/_4$ Br. tbsp.) Dijon mustard
pepper and salt to taste
$^1/_2$ cup (4 fl. oz.) minced onion
2 tbsp. ($1$ $^1/_2$ Br. tbsp.) freshly chopped dill

Scrub potatoes. Cover with water; bring to boil and cook until pierced easily with a fork. Drain; cool under cold running water. Let stand for 15 minutes. Cube potatoes, then place in a large bowl. Toss with oil and vinegar. Make dressing by mixing together mayonnaise, yogurt, mustard, salt, and pepper. Stir in the onion and dill, then pour mixture over potatoes. Toss. Cover and chill before serving.

*Every one must have felt that a cheerful friend is like a sunny day, which sheds its brightness on all around . . .*
　　　　　　　　　　　　　　　　　*—Lord Avebury*

# Vinaigrette Salad

1 large cucumber
2 medium tomatoes
2 small green peppers
1 small onion
dash of garlic powder
half a head of cauliflower
1 cup (8 fl. oz.) salad oil

⅓ cup (2 ½ fl. oz.)
   tarragon vinegar
2 tsp. (1 ½ Br. tsp.)
   oregano
1 tsp. (¾ Br. tsp.) parsley
½ tsp. each dry mustard,
   salt, and pepper

Chop or slice vegetables. Place in glass or ceramic container. Whisk together the oil, vinegar, herbs, and spices. Pour dressing over vegetables; stir. Cover; chill for 2-3 hours, stirring occasionally. Serve on beds of leaf lettuce.

# Stir-Fried Broccoli

1 ½ lbs. broccoli, washed
   and drained
2 tbsp. (1 ½ Br. tbsp.) extra
   virgin olive oil
¼ tsp. minced garlic

¾ cup (6 fl. oz.) grated
   Feta cheese
1 tsp. (¾ Br. tsp.) oregano
1 tbsp. (¾ Br. tbsp.) lemon
   juice

*It is a friendly heart that has plenty of friends.*
—William Makepeace Thackeray

Cut broccoli into bite-size pieces, separating stem and floret pieces and removing any tough, fibrous peel from stems. Heat olive oil in a heavy wok or skillet until very hot. Sauté stems for 3 to 4 minutes. Add florets; sauté for 2 to 3 minutes. Stir in cheese, herbs, and lemon juice. Heat through and serve immediately.

ONE OF THE PLEASANTEST THINGS IN THE WORLD IS GOING A~JOURNEY.

## Spaghetti with Pesto

4 cloves garlic
hot cooked spaghetti
2 ½ cups (1 Br. pt.) chopped
   fresh basil
½ cup (4 fl. oz.) virgin olive
   oil
⅓ cup (2 ½ fl. oz.) lightly
   toasted pine nuts

½ cup (4 fl. oz.) grated
   Parmesan and pecorino
   Romano cheese
½ cup (4 fl. oz.) sun-dried
   tomatoes, cut in small
   pieces
additional lightly toasted
   pine nuts

Blend or process all ingredients except pasta and
tomatoes. Toss hot spaghetti, tomatoes, and
additional pine nuts with the sauce.

*There's nothing half so pleasant*
*As coming home again.*
*—Margaret Sangster*

# Rotini Salad

8 ounces rotini (cooked, drained,
    and cooled)
$^1/_2$ cup (4 fl. oz.) olive oil
2 tbsp. (1 $^1/_2$ Br. tbsp.) lemon juice
$^1/_2$ tsp. ground black pepper
$^1/_4$ tsp. dried oregano
$^1/_8$ tsp. garlic powder
12 cherry tomatoes, halved
2 green peppers, cut in slivers
10 black olives, pitted and halved
10 radishes, thinly sliced
1 small cucumber, chopped
2 tbsp. (1 $^1/_2$ Br. tbsp.) sliced
    green onion
2 tbsp. (1 $^1/_2$ Br. tbsp.) chopped
    fresh parsley
4 ounces crumbled Feta cheese

Combine oil, lemon juice, pepper, oregano, and
garlic; blend thoroughly and chill. Toss remaining
ingredients in a large bowl. Add the dressing, then
toss lightly and serve.

*When love and skill work together, expect a
masterpiece.*
                                        —John Ruskin

# Spinach Pasta Salad

*8 ounces spinach noodles*
*1 cup (8 fl. oz.) cauliflower florets,*
*steamed until just tender*
*1 cup (8 fl. oz.) sliced mushrooms*
*1/2 cup (4 fl. oz.) Italian dressing*
*1 cup (8 fl. oz.) cooked ham, thinly*
*sliced and cut in narrow strips*
*1/2 cup (4 fl. oz.) grated Parmesan*
*cheese*

Cook noodles until just tender; drain well. In a large bowl combine cauliflower, mushrooms, and dressing. Add warm noodles and ham; toss lightly. Spoon into serving bowls; sprinkle with Parmesan and serve.

*A good heart is better than all the heads in the world.*

—Edward Bulwer-Lytton

## Chicken Limón

*2 whole boned chicken breasts*
*flour, garlic powder, salt, and pepper*
*3 tbsp. (2 ¹/₄ Br. tbsp.) olive oil*
*¹/₂ cup (4 fl. oz.) finely chopped onion*
*some sliced mushrooms*
*2 tbsp. (1 ¹/₂ Br. tbsp.) lemon juice*
*³/₄ cup (6 fl. oz.) white wine*
*³/₄ cup (6 fl. oz.) chicken bouillon*

Trim breasts and split them. Season flour with garlic powder, salt, and pepper; dredge the breasts in flour mixture. Brown them in the oil until cooked. Remove to a plate. Cook the onion and mushrooms in the oil until tender. Add lemon juice, wine, and bouillon; put the chicken back in the pan. Boil until most of the wine cooks off and the sauce thickens a bit. Serve with rice.

*Sit down and feed, and welcome to our table.*
—William Shakespeare

## Steak with Savory Sauce

Cut a 1-lb. sirloin steak into quarters; pound pieces until thin. In a heavy skillet heat 2 tbsp. (1 1/2 Br. tbsp.) olive oil over medium heat. Sauté steak for 5 minutes on each side. Remove from skillet; keep warm. Add 2 tbsp. more olive oil to skillet. Sauté 1 cup (8 fl. oz.) sliced onion and 1/2 cup (4 fl. oz.) chopped mushrooms until tender. Add 4 tbsp. (3 Br. tbsp.) red wine vinegar, 4 tsp. (3 Br. tsp.) Dijon mustard, 1/4 cup (2 fl. oz.) beef broth, and 1/2 tsp. pepper to skillet. Stir sauce for 2 minutes; serve over steak.

*Guard within yourself that treasure, kindness.*
—George Sand

# Tuna-Cashew Casserole

3-ounce can chow mein noodles
1 can (about 10 fl. oz.) condensed
  cream of mushroom soup
6- to 9-ounce can white tuna,
  drained and flaked
1/4 lb. chopped cashew nuts (salted
  or unsalted)
1 cup (8 fl. oz.) diced celery
4 tbsp. (3 Br. tbsp.) chopped onion
1/4 cup (2 fl. oz.) water
1/2 tsp. salt
1/8 tsp. pepper

Save 1/2 cup (4 fl. oz.) noodles to sprinkle over top
of casserole. Mix together rest of ingredients. Pour
into a greased 1-quart (32 fl. oz.) casserole dish or
into 6 individual shells. Sprinkle reserved noodles
over top. Bake casserole at 325° F for 40 minutes
(or individual shells for 25 minutes). Makes 6
 servings.

*Better a good dinner than a fine coat.*
*—Proverb*

# Oriental Stir-Fry

6 ounces fine egg noodles
2 tbsp. (1 ½ Br. tbsp.) safflower oil
½ cup each: bamboo shoots,
    sliced mushrooms, slivered
    almonds, sliced water chestnuts,
    and cooked chicken or shrimp
2 green onions or scallions,
    finely chopped
¾ cup (6 fl. oz.) chicken broth
2 tbsp. (1 ½ Br. tbsp.) soy sauce

Cook noodles; drain well. Heat oil over low heat in wok or large skillet. Stir-fry the noodles for 3 to 4 minutes, stirring constantly. Add vegetables, nuts, and meat, then stir in broth and soy sauce. Cover; simmer on low heat until liquid is almost absorbed. Serve hot.

*Happy is the house that shelters a friend.*
*—Ralph Waldo Emerson*

## Margie's Cheesecake

*Crust:*
1 cup (8 fl. oz.) graham cracker
    (digestive biscuit) crumbs
¹/₄ cup (2 fl. oz.) sugar
¹/₂ tsp. cinnamon
¹/₄ cup (2 fl. oz.) melted butter

*Filling:*
1 lb. cream cheese
¹/₂ cup (4 fl. oz.) sugar
3 eggs

*Topping:*
1 pt. (16 fl. oz.) sour cream
¹/₄ cup (2 fl. oz.) sugar
1 tsp. (³/₄ Br. tsp.) vanilla extract

Combine crust mixture; spread in a springform (loose bottom) pan. Beat filling ingredients until smooth; put on top of crust. Bake 20 minutes at 375° F. Let cool for 1 hour. Combine topping ingredients and put on top of filling. Bake another 10 minutes at 475° F. Top with whipped cream before serving.

*Part of the secret of success in life is to eat what you like . . .*
—Mark Twain

30

# Mocha Dream Brownies

$^1/_4$ lb. softened butter
$^1/_2$ lb. softened cream cheese
1 $^1/_2$ cups (12 fl. oz.) sugar
3 eggs
1 tsp. ($^3/_4$ Br. tsp.) instant
    coffee powder
2 tsp. (1 $^1/_2$ Br. tsp.) hot water
$^3/_4$ cup (6 fl. oz.) flour
$^1/_2$ cup (4 fl. oz.) unsweetened
    cocoa powder
$^1/_2$ tsp. salt
2 tsp. (1 $^1/_2$ Br. tsp.) vanilla extract
1 cup (8 fl. oz.) chopped walnuts

Heat oven to 350° F. Grease a 9-inch square pan.
Cream butter with cream cheese. Add sugar; beat
well. One ingredient at a time, beat in remaining
ingredients. Pour batter into greased pan. Bake 30
minutes. Cut into squares.

*Where we love is home,*
*Home that our feet may leave,*
*but not our hearts.*
    *—Oliver Wendell Holmes*

# Mary's Gooey Butter Coffee Cake

1 Betty Crocker pound cake mix
2 eggs
¹/₄ lb. margarine, melted
2 tbsp. (1 ¹/₂ Br. tbsp.) vanilla
    extract
1 box (1 lb.) confectioners' sugar,
    with 2 tbsp. (1 ¹/₂ Br. tbsp.) held back

Blend the first 3 ingredients and place in a large ungreased oven-proof glass baking dish. Mix the last 2 ingredients and pour on top. Bake 15 minutes at 300° F and then add the reserved confectioners' sugar and bake an additional 25 minutes.

*The love we give away is the only love we keep.*
—Elbert Hubbard

# Fudge

2 cups (16 fl. oz.) sugar
2 ½ tbsp. (1 ¾ Br. tbsp.) cocoa
1 cup (8 fl. oz.) milk
2 tbsp. (1 ½ Br. tbsp.) butter
1 ½ tsp. (1 Br. tsp.) vanilla extract
chopped pecans (optional)

Mix sugar, cocoa, and milk in medium saucepan and stir to boiling point. Reduce heat and bring to soft ball stage. Remove from heat; add butter and vanilla. Beat with spoon until fudge thickens. Pour onto greased platter, adding pecans before pouring, if desired. Cut into squares.

*Every house where love abides,*
*And friendship is a guest,*
*Is surely home, and home-sweet-home:*
*For there the heart can rest.*
*—Henry van Dyke*

WE CANNOT TELL THE PRECISE MOMENT WHEN FRIENDSHIP IS FORMED. AS IN FILLING A VESSEL DROP BY DROP, THERE IS AT LAST A DROP WHICH MAKES IT RUN OVER; SO IN A SERIES OF KINDNESSES THERE IS AT LAST ONE WHICH MAKES THE HEART RUN OVER.

····· JAMES BOSWELL

# ❧ TEATIME TIDBITS ❧

## Spiced Tea

4 cups (32 fl. oz.) boiling water
4 tsp. (3 Br. tsp.) loose black tea
1/4 tsp. crushed whole cloves
1/8 tsp. cinnamon
1/2 tsp. dried orange peel
1/2 cup (4 fl. oz.) orange juice
1 tbsp. (3/4 Br. tbsp.) lemon juice
1/4 cup (2 fl. oz.) sugar

Place tea, cloves, cinnamon, and orange peel in teapot. Pour boiling water into pot. Cover; let steep 3 to 5 minutes. Meanwhile heat sugar, orange juice, and lemon juice to boiling. Stir; add to hot tea and stir. Strain and pour.

*Tea Tip: Brew tea as usual, but instead of adding sugar or honey to sweeten, stir a teaspoon or two of fruit preserves into the cup. Strawberry, cherry, and apricot are especially good.*

*Thank God for tea! What would the world do without tea?—how did it exist? I am glad I was not born before tea.*

—Sydney Smith

# Lemon Squares

2 cups (16 fl. oz.) flour
1/2 cup (4 fl. oz.)
    confectioners' sugar
1/2 lb. melted butter
4 eggs
2 cups (16 fl. oz.)
    granulated sugar
6 tbsp. (4 1/2 Br. tbsp.)
    lemon juice
4 tbsp. (3 Br. tbsp.) flour
1/2 tsp. baking powder

Line a 13-inch by 9-inch pan with aluminum foil.
Mix 2 cups flour, confectioners' sugar, and butter;
press into pan. Bake at 350° F for 20 minutes. Mix
eggs, granulated sugar, juice, 4 tbsp. flour, and
baking powder; pour over crust. Bake for 25
minutes at 350° F. Sprinkle with confectioners'
sugar. Cool; cut into squares.

*Tea Tip: Instead of using water to brew tea, use apple juice that
has been heated to a boil. This may be served hot or chilled over
ice. Earl Grey tea is especially delicious when brewed this way.*

*The ornament of a house is the friends who frequent it.*
—Ralph Waldo Emerson

# Tea Sandwiches

Spread the cut face of a loaf of bread with softened butter or cream cheese before cutting off each slice. Slice bread thinly, trim off crusts, fill sandwiches, then cut into triangles or fingers.
Suggested Fillings:

*1) Butter blended with fresh chopped watercress leaves*

*2) Cream cheese with either fresh chopped chives, nuts, pineapple, olives, or cooked shrimp*

*3) Butter with chopped cooked lobster and watercress leaves; or butter with mashed cooked salmon and chopped cucumber; add mayonnaise and lemon juice to these mixtures to moisten*

*Tea Tip: To flavor iced tea, dilute 2 tbsp. (1 ¹/₂ Br. tbsp.) lemon juice or 4 tbsp. (3 Br. tbsp.) other fruit juice with enough water to fill an ice cube tray. Freeze, then use the ice cubes in glasses of tea.*

*Little deeds of kindness, little words of love,*
*Help to make earth happy like the heaven above.*
*—Julia Fletcher Carney*

DO UNTO OTHERS AS YOU WOULD HAVE THEM DO UNTO YOU

FOR ME??!

38

# Chocolate Meringues

*½ cup (4 fl. oz.) cocoa powder*
*½ cup (4 fl. oz.) sugar*
*⅛ tsp. mace*
*3 egg whites*

Heat oven to 325° F. Grease a baking or cookie sheet. Sift together the cocoa powder, sugar, and mace. Beat egg whites until stiff. Gently blend egg whites into cocoa mixture with a fork, but do not overstir. Drop mixture by teaspoonfuls onto baking sheet, leaving 2 inches between spoonfuls. Bake about 10 minutes or until set. Remove from sheet at once and cool on a wire rack.

*One of the most beautiful qualities of true friendship is to understand and to be understood.*

—Seneca

# ❧ GIFTS FROM THE ❧ KITCHEN AND GARDEN

*Use the following ideas and recipes to indulge yourself with a simple pleasure or to create a thoughtful gift for a friend. For presenting to a friend, place the item in a decorative basket or tin, or a bottle tied with a ribbon.*

## Citrus and Spice Potpourri

To add a pleasant fragrance to the kitchen after cooking foods with strong odors, try the following mixture. In a large bowl combine: dried lemon peel, dried orange peel, broken cinnamon sticks, crushed ginger, crushed nutmeg, whole cloves, and whole allspice. Place a few teaspoonfuls of the mixture in a tea ball. Submerge the ball in a saucepan of water; bring water to boil. Reduce heat; simmer so scent fills the room. (For giving to a friend, sew the mixture into little muslin bags tied with a string.)

Or to scent a room area, peel 6 oranges and 3 lemons, tearing the peel into 1-inch pieces. Push a few whole cloves into each piece. Air-dry in a flat container, then place in a decorative basket or bowl in the room. Stir to activate scent.

■ ■ ■ ■ ■ ■ ■ ■ ■ ■ ■ ■ ■ ■

*What brings joy to the heart is not so much the friend's gift as the friend's love.*

—Aelred of Rievaulx

# Lavender Oil

Collect lavender flowers and leaves; place in a wide-mouthed jar. Fill the jar with an unscented or pure oil, such as sesame or almond oil. Let stand in a warm place for 24 hours, then strain the oil through cheesecloth. Add fresh flowers and leaves to strained oil. Keep repeating the process until the oil has a strong scent. Strain and filter into a bottle with a tight cap. Use as a personal fragrance or for scenting potpourri.

# Herb-Infused Oil

In a sterilized bottle, place a garlic clove, several sprigs of washed and dried oregano, and a long strip of lemon peel. Fill almost to top with olive oil. Cap and store in refrigerator for 10 days. Bring to room temperature before using. Use in salad dressing or to brush on poultry or fish before baking or broiling.

*Not what we give, but what we share,*
*For the gift without the giver is bare ...*
*—James Russell Lowell*

# Bouquets Garnis

For each bouquet, cut a 4-inch square of double-thick cheesecloth. Place ingredients in center of square and tie together with white string. Store in tightly closed containers in a cool, dry place. (For giving bouquets garnis to a friend, put them in a little basket or tin, with labels for their use.)

Beef/Pork: *1 tsp. (³/₄ Br. tsp.) each summer savory, thyme, marjoram, parsley, sage, celery seed, and grated lemon peel, plus 2 crushed bay leaves*

Chicken/Fish: *1 tsp. (³/₄ Br. tsp.) each chervil, chives, tarragon, and grated lemon peel*

Soups/Stews: *1 tsp. (³/₄ Br. tsp.) each thyme, basil, marjoram, rosemary, and parsley, plus 1 peeled garlic clove and 6 peppercorns*

# Raspberry Vinegar

Fill a sterilized bottle one-quarter full of fresh raspberries and juice. Pour in distilled white vinegar until almost full. Seal; store for at least 2 weeks in refrigerator before using as a salad dressing or marinade.

*The only gift is a portion of thyself.*
—*Ralph Waldo Emerson*

SOW GOOD SERVICES; SWEET REMEMBRANCES WILL GROW FROM THEM.

Mde. de Stael

43

# Basil Vinegar

Wash several sprigs of freshly picked basil. Let dry completely, then put in a sterilized bottle. Pour in cider vinegar or red wine vinegar until almost full. Seal; let stand for 1 to 2 weeks before using. This blend is delicious on fresh tomatoes.

# Tea Blends

Thoroughly dry any herbs, flowers, or fruit peel for these blends. Crush herbs, removing stems. Use 1 tsp. ($^3/_4$ Br. tsp.) per cup of boiling water. (For giving to a friend, put loose tea in a decorative tin and present with a tea ball.) Try the following combinations in any desired proportion: lemon peel, bergamot, and spearmint; orange pekoe tea, orange peel, and whole cloves; and rose hips, hibiscus, lemon grass, lemon peel, and orange peel.

*Give what you have. To some one, it may be better than you dare to think.*
—*Henry Wadsworth Longfellow*

Mary Engelbreit is an internationally recognized artist and designer, whose work combines warmth, wit, nostalgia, and a unique style. Born and raised in a St. Louis, Missouri suburb, her artistic talent surfaced early. Though mostly self-taught, she attended summer art classes as a teenager. After several years working as a commercial illustrator, Mary signed with Portal Publications, where she established a national reputation. She started her own greeting card company, which she eventually sold to Sunrise Publications. Since 1982 she has developed a strong licensing program. Her designs appear on a wide variety of products, including tins, mugs, plates, Christmas ornaments, picture frames, clothing, and textiles. Mary still lives and works in St. Louis with her husband and two young sons.